D1542587

IMAGES OF
SPAIN

IMAGES OF
SPAIN

XAN FIELDING

Bounty Books

San Vicente The sun rises over the
Ebro valley and the hilltop church of
San Vicente, La Rioja

First published in 1991 by Hamlyn, an imprint
of Octopus Publishing Group Ltd

This edition published 2005 by Bounty Books,
a division of Octopus Publishing Group Ltd
2–4 Heron Quays, London E14 4JP

Copyright © Octopus Publishing Group Ltd

All rights reserved. No part of this work may be
reproduced or utilized in any form or by any
means, electronic or mechanical, including
photocopying, recording or by any information
storage and retrieval system, without the prior
written permission of the publisher

ISBN 0 7537 1233 4
ISBN13 9780753712337

A CIP catalogue record for this book is available
from the British Library

Printed and bound in China

Introduction

The first night I spent in Spain, nearly forty years ago, was in a hotel facing the cathedral in Barcelona. Looking out from my balcony at sunset I was conscious of something in the air, a sense of expectancy that seemed to emanate from the crowd in the square below, and presently I noticed that an eleven-man band had assembled on the perron. The music started up – thin reedy notes which might have issued from Pan-pipes rather than from the instruments being played – and for a while nothing happened. Then, as the tempo quickened, the crowd spontaneously dissolved into separate fragments, each of which in turn became a circle of individuals, hands joined with arms outstretched, treading a measure that looked as rustic and antique as the accompaniment sounded. It was as though the interlocking hoops of several Olympic Games emblems had incongruously come apart. Each circumference pulsated, without revolving, round a central pile of discarded jackets and handbags and shoes doffed in favour of espadrilles. From time to time a passer-by would duck under a bridge of arms, add his or her contribution to the pile, and then join the circle; or else, in reverse, would break the circle, leaving a momentary gap, retrieve what he or she had deposited, then duck back under the bridge and wander off. It was an absorbing and ever-changing pattern. I did not know *at the time that I was watching the* sardana, *a harvest dance handed down from Homeric times, now the national dance of Catalonia.*

Long after it was over, when the band had packed up and the dancers had dispersed, I stayed on my balcony pondering the impromptu entertainment and gazing at the cathedral, which darkness gradually turned into a silhouette. I had no idea I was in for another treat, but suddenly it happened. Some municipal or ecclesiastical finger somewhere tripped a switch, illuminating the stained glass windows from within and the spire and the façade from without. Simultaneously the gulls perching on every sill and finial took wing, seemingly like doves, feathered phantoms in a nocturnal aerial display. My most vivid memory of Spain for many years was that flight of paracletes, that drifting, dipping, soaring, spinning multitude of Holy Ghosts.

In time the vision dimmed, and others, more or less dazzling, superimposed themselves upon it after I came to live here; but it continued to reside in the depths of my consciousness. I made no attempt to bring it to the surface, for to try to recapture a moment of bliss is to court disappointment. But one evening I found myself back in Barcelona, and staying at the same hotel. I looked out from my balcony at sunset – and stepped into a time warp.

It was as though the intervening quarter of a century had never been. An eleven-man cobla *(yes, I had since learnt what this curious* sardana *band is called) was again assembling on the perron, and now I could distinguish some of the instruments: flageolet, tambourine, trombone, double bass, a couple of oboes. The music started up, and the square was again patterned with pulsating circles that expanded or contracted each time a dancer linked up or withdrew. And later, as darkness fell and the cathedral lights came on, the dove-like gulls celebrated once again their nightly Pentecost.*

The birds' display was as brilliant as I remembered, but what struck me more was the sense of continuity engendered by the human activity earlier on. The sardana was clearly no mere relic from the past, kept alive by the elderly and middle-aged; there had been just as many youngsters taking part. Clad in uniform blue jeans, T-shirts and trainers, and crowned with unisex haircuts which blurred the distinction between girl and boy, they looked more suited to the psychedelic pandemonium of a discothèque than to the bucolic-bourgeois gaiety of the cathedral square. Yet they were no less adept than their elders at the delicate, intricate footwork demanded by their national dance; it was second nature to them, it was in their blood. Unconsciously they were celebrating a ritual, subscribing, willy-nilly, to a tradition.

Every region of Spain has a dance of its own. Some are of great antiquity: the Basque carrica is said to be a remnant of the Iberian tripudium, which Hannibal had performed at the funeral of the consul Tiberius Gracchus; and 'Morris' dances took place in Galicia long before John of Gaunt imported them to England. Then there are the 'roundabout' rondallas of Valencia, the habas verdes ('broad beans') of León, the jota of Aragón, the seguidilla of La Mancha, the bolero and fandango of Andalucía... Where these have survived, they have survived intact, and are still performed spontaneously, for their own delight, by the inhabitants of their places of origin. Gypsy flamenco is something else again. It survives, to be sure, and occurs all over

Andalucía. But it has also become theatrical entertainment, vulgarised and debased for the benefit of foreign tourists. Grotesque performances can be seen any day in any boite on every costa, punctuated by cries of Olé! uttered in a variety of accents other than Spanish and therefore sounding, to the ear of an Anglophone, more like an exhortation to a recalcitrant hen than an expression of the audience's enthusiasm.

Is it over-fanciful to equate these dances with aspects of the Spanish way of life, in which the dignified and traditional predominate over the brash and the 'progressive'? How long this will last, there's no telling. Already, more than once, the balance has been alternately disturbed and restored. For some time after Franco's death, permissiveness ran riot. Cinemas showed nothing but hard porn. I once went to an afternoon session in the little town of Cazorla, and was faced with scene after scene portraying acts of gross indecency. But to judge by the reaction of the spectators, among whom I noticed several family parties and even a priest or two, they might have been watching the dullest of documentaries. There was no exclamation of dismay, no titter of embarrassment, let alone a prurient guffaw. And as they filed out after the performance, no blush mantled any cheek. Indifference, if not boredom, was the pervading sensation. Everyone, not only in Cazorla but all over Spain, had had a surfeit of this diet; a change was needed, and in due course occurred.

To the question 'Has modern civilization reached Spain at last?' I might be tempted to reply, 'Yes, of course. People are now mugged in the streets in broad daylight. You can't stroll through a public park without stubbing your toe on a hypodermic. The papers are full of advertisements for massage parlours... It's just like the rest of Europe.'

But of course it isn't. Certainly petty crime is on the increase – Seville, of all places, swarms with pickpockets and bagsnatchers – and corruption in official circles is daily reported in the press. But only a bigot blinded by nostalgia for the recent past, when Spain was a byword for honesty, would have cause to bewail the difference between then and now. Certainly, too, the use of drugs is spreading; but not enough for a would-be guardian of public morals to have an excuse for comparing, to the latter's detriment, the Spain of yesterday to today's. And massage parlours are indeed a novelty, but only as a euphemism for something that existed already: prostitution has always featured in Spanish life. Even Franco was unable to prevent the streetwalkers of Barcelona from plying their trade openly on the ramblas; he could only, by outlawing Catalan, stop them soliciting in their native language.

So, on second thoughts, I would have to admit that for all her belated entry into the twentieth century, for all the lip-service she pays to modernity, for all her lately acquired affluence and her vulnerability to materialism and consumerism of the flashiest kind, Spain is still her old self: individualist, independent, fatalistic and hostile to regimentation (sometimes even to new ideas). Burros may now be out-numbered by motorbikes and jeeps, and ox-drawn ploughs superseded by tractors, but not a day passes without my being reminded of a civilization based until very recently on the luxury of leisure more than on creature comforts. I don't think Spain will ever be able, or willing, to break with her past.

Northern Spain

Spain is not one but several. The present Kingdom is a conglomeration of former kingdoms – not for nothing did the Catholic Monarchs call themselves los Reyes de las Españas, 'the King and Queen of the Spains' – and each has its own regional identity. Rather than deal with them individually, however, I have found it more convenient to divide the country into four distinctive regions based more or less on the cardinal points of the compass. The illustrations that follow are therefore grouped in separate sections corresponding to those regions, with a fifth devoted to the islands: the Canaries and the Balearics. Let us then, as though reading the Peninsula like the page of a book, start at the top left-hand corner and make our way eastward between the sea and the Cantabrian mountains, from the Kingdom of Galicia, through the principality of Asturias and the Basque provinces, and on to the kingdoms of Navarra and Aragón. We shall thus travel right across the first of my chosen regions – Northern Spain.

We shall also be following, but in the opposite direction, the final section of the Way of St James, the road trodden by hundreds of thousands of medieval pilgrims heading for Santiago de Compostela. In fact they had more than one way of entering Spain from France. They could cross the Pyrenees over the Roncesvalles pass and march inland south of the mountains; or else skirt the French and then the Spanish coast, at the risk of being attacked from the sea by Barbary pirates. Either way, they found themselves in a land totally at variance with the traditional image of Spain.

In Galicia, a Portuguese would be on immediate speaking terms with the inhabitants, his language being closely akin to theirs. An Irishman would find much in common with his native island, not least the verdure of the small-holdings due to the heavy rainfall. The sound of bagpipes, which are played in no other region of Spain, would remind a Scotsman of the Highlands; as would the steep granite sierras. Gazing at the upland pastures, a Swiss might fancy himself back in the Alps. And a Norwegian would instinctively compare the rías – those long narrow arms of the sea tunnelling into the coast – to Trondheim or any other fjord.

In Asturias, too, and in the rest of the Northern Zone, there is much with which foreigners would be familiar. In Navarra and Aragón they would find the salmon rivers and trout streams not so very different from those on the other side of the Pyrenees and, with a smattering of Spanish, they would be able to converse with the locals. But they would be lost in the Basque country whose language resembles no other and where the inhabitants, according to Castilian-speakers, write 'Solomon' and pronounce it 'Nebuchadnezzar.'

The Way of St James

Give me my scallop-shell of quiet,
My bottle of salvation,
My staff of faith to walk upon,
My gown of glory, hope's true gage,
My scrip of joy, immortal diet,
And thus I'll take my pilgrimage.

Sir Walter Raleigh

Pilgrims of today still wear the emblem of St James on the road to Santiago de Compostela. In some cases, however, the scallop-shell is manifestly not of quiet; and banners and flags are more in evidence than the staff of faith.

Santiago de Compostela Country
churches along the pilgrims' route
bear an echo or foretaste of the great
cathedral at journey's end. Here a
dazzling spectacle awaits them.
Santiago's censer, the famous
botafumeiro, is so heavy that it takes
eight specially trained men to get it
moving. By skilful manipulation of
ropes and pulleys they swing it in ever
widening arcs until it reaches the
roof, whence it comes zooming down,
dive-bombing the congregation with
sparks from the charcoal-fired incense
inside it, before soaring roofwards
again in the opposite direction.

The Picos de Europa A funicular and a ring road have opened up the Picos to a new sort of visitor: transistor-toting picnickers as heedless of the noise they make as of the litter they leave behind. Fortunately, they don't venture far from the cable-car or their own motor-cars; so on the whole these Asturian highlands, the most dramatic section of the Cantabrian range, remain unsullied. The steepest peaks are inaccessible to all but the most experienced mountaineer; but with a little effort anyone can climb high enough to be rewarded, if he is lucky, with the sight of chamoix scampering about or, even if out of luck, with an unforgettable panorama.

Castro Urdiales So bad at one time was the bridle road between Santander and Bilbao, that people preferred to travel by sea from the one town to the other. Yet seamen were wary of this iron-bound coast on which the Atlantic boils and thunders, and grateful for such havens as Castro Urdiales. Storm-tossed in the Bay of Biscay, they would murmur, '*A Castro o al Cielo* – to Castro or to heaven.' The beautifully situated little port still depends for its livelihood on fishing and canning, which with any luck may save it from becoming a fashionable seaside resort.

Ainsa There was a time when every community in the Aragonese highlands lived isolated in its own valley, making do with the simple pleasures of a pastoral existence and putting up with the hardships. Then came the hydro-electric works, the dams and artificial lakes, the metalled roads and public transport, which turned that existence topsy-turvy. Many inhabitants of such picturesque villages as Ainsa went off to work in the nearest towns and those who remained installed running water and other amenities in their stone-walled, slate-roofed houses, fortunately without altering their character.

Sos del Rey Católico The reek of history that emanates from this little Aragonese town is not due only to its renown as the birthplace of Ferdinand the Catholic. It dates back to the Middle Ages, as its well-preserved walls and gateways proclaim. Nothing could be more different from it than the village of Alloza (*right*) in the southern part of this kingdom of contrasts. Too far from the Ebro to benefit from irrigation, it rises like a heap of rubble from a table-land reminiscent of the Steppes.

The Pyrenees *'Il n'y a plus de Pyrénées* – the Pyrenees have ceased to exist,' said Louis XIV at the accession of his grandson to the throne of Spain. Just a figure of speech, of course, but it can now be taken literally; for what can be easier than burrowing under the great range through either of the two road tunnels or climbing over it by any of the dozen or so motorable passes? To cross the Pyrenees on foot and off the macadam is the only way to appreciate their grandeur to the full; euphoria and a sense of achievement enhancing the landscape at every step.

Pamplona As anyone who has read Ernest Hemingway's *The Sun Also Rises* will know, the bullrunning that takes place at Pamplona during the Feria de San Fermín has nothing to do with bullfighting. Six bulls and six big oxen are released from a corral into barricaded streets leading to the bullring. They gallop along this improvised race-track with hundreds of young men running just ahead of them. As the animals are faster than the humans, there are some spectacular accidents and pile-ups. A heifer is finally let loose on the crowd in the arena. The event has drawn increasingly large numbers of foreigners since Hemingway and his fictional characters discovered it nearly seven decades ago.

San Sebastián (*following pages*)
Spain's counterpart of Biarritz owes
its aura of old-world elegance to the
patronage of two Spanish queens.
Isabel II put it on the map by
holidaying there in 1845; soon
afterwards it became the summer
residence of the court, the
government and most of the
aristocracy. Then, in 1912, María
Cristina inaugurated the grand hotel
named after her. It is still considered
the queen of hotels on the northern
Spanish coast, haunted by ghosts of
the *belle époque* and frequented by
starlets attending the San Sebastián
Film Festival.

Central Spain

I have expanded the frontiers of Central Spain so as to embrace Extremadura as well as the two Castiles, Old and New – lately renamed, for some arcane administrative purpose, Castilla-León and Castilla-La Mancha. This former dual kingdom is the heart and citadel of the country, the cradle of the nation, and it lent its 'canting' name to the Spanish language: 'Castilla' was taken from the number of castles erected here in defence against the Moors. Diehard Castilians have always considered themselves a cut above the rest of Spain – to them, Africa begins on the Guadiana – and even those of humble birth feel equal to the proudest noble. In their eyes to be Castilian is to be a gentleman, a hidalgo, 'a son of a somebody.' This may be why Castilians – indeed Spaniards in general – are blessedly free from class-consciousness; master and servant are to this day in as natural a relationship as Don Quixote and Sancho Panza.

But I won't let the Castiles have it all their own way. Extremadura has equal reason to be proud, in fact all the more for having always been so poor. No other province has produced so many conquistadors – men like Pizarro, the illiterate son of a penniless swineherd, who went West to make good and to earn, incidentally, a reputation for bestial cruelty. If he really was as beastly as some people make out, it's no doubt because he was suckled – though this may be just another legend – not like Romulus and Remus by a she-wolf, but by an Extremadurian sow.

Madrid A traffic jam at three o'clock in the morning, a not uncommon occurrence, is an indication of the capital's life-style. Madrid is a city not of noctambulists (for the whole place is wide-awake as well as on the go) but of night-owls in human form.

Madrid Daytime in Madrid is no less frenzied: the rush hour is at all hours. What makes this bearable is the attitude of the inhabitants. *Madrileños* may have plenty to complain about in the way of over-crowding and pollution, but they also have plenty to be pleased with and to be proud of, not least a sense of civic stimulation and personal well-being. It is not a question of their loving the place for better or for worse; what matters more is that they enjoy it.

The Retiro Madrid's oldest and
largest park outdoes London's Hyde
Park in one respect at least: it still has
its Crystal Palace. It also has an
equivalent to the Serpentine – the
Estanque where rowers take to the
waters on Sunday afternoons. In the
climate of Castile – *'tres meses de
invierno, y nueve de infierno,'*
'three months of winter, nine of hell'
– water and shade are as welcome as
a bench in the sun.

The Escorial This vast palace-cum-monastery-cum-mausoleum, built by Philip II and dedicated to St. Lawrence, expresses in its austerity and vigour two essential Spanish characteristics. The clear-cut pattern of the building is gridiron-shaped, in tribute to the saint who was martyred by being roasted alive. From here the pious and ascetic king of what was then the richest and most powerful nation on earth boasted of 'ruling half the world with two inches of paper.' But when he died, in 1598, it was not in the odour of sanctity but in the stink of his own putrescence, and in the knowledge that Spain's empire was already crumbling.

Segovia It's as hard to imagine Segovia without its aqueduct as to picture Paris without the Eiffel Tower. This masterpiece of Roman engineering is the emblem of that typically Castilian city, and each complements and enhances the other. Built of granite without cement or mortar, the noble structure combines simplicity, proportion, solidity and utility. It would dwarf or diminish most surroundings; but Segovia, standing on a natural rampart, literally soars above it, sometimes seeming to float across the landscape like a galleon in full sail.

The Windmills of La Mancha
(preceding pages) Here are three of
the 'giants' chosen by Don Quixote
as targets for his lance. Thanks to
Cervantes, no one even now can cross
this arid tableland without thinking
of the Knight of the Rueful Counte-
nance. The actual inhabitants are
more prosaic – makers of Valdepeñas
wine and bland *manchego* cheese –
but the Don lives on in their hearts
and in their minds, the quintessential
Spaniard, courageous, romantic and
mystical. Long may he survive.

The Great Central Plain In most
parts of Spain agriculture has been
mechanized; but in the poorer
villages threshing and winnowing are
still performed by hand and with
hand-made tools. Here, in the
patchwork fields of Extremadura,
women thresh lentils. Who's to tell,
however, how much longer the
primitive and picturesque will hold
out against the labour-saving and
convenient?

The Monastery of Guadalupe
(*preceding pages*) Like so many other shrines all over Spain, Guadalupe owes its existence to a statuette of the Virgin that was hidden away at the time of the Muslim invasion and rediscovered by chance centuries later. That such an unassuming little effigy should give rise to the vast edifice that now contains it, is really no more strange than that an acorn should sprout into an oak. Yet there must have been something special about Our Lady of Guadalupe. Why else would Columbus have named an island after Her, or the Conquistadors revered Her as the symbol of *La Hispanidad*?

Toledo From certain angles, when you look at Toledo from a distance, you still see what El Greco saw when he first settled here. So little has the city changed in the intervening years, and so enduring is the impact of the painter's view of it, that even on a clear day your mind's eye fills the sky above it with his storm-clouds, as though a harsher climate was needed to intensify the severity of those battlements and towers. Within the walls, too, fair weather might seem out of place; but it is not on that account but because of the heat of the sun that the narrow streets are shaded by awnings.

Extremadura (*preceding pages*)
This is Spain's 'Empty Quarter', so
underpopulated that when you come
across a sign of human habitation
you feel like an explorer discovering
the black tents of a lost nomadic
tribe. But Extremadura is no
wilderness. Under skies patrolled by
eagles there are meadowlands filled
with cork trees, and hillsides aromatic
with cystus and peony which recall
the Hymn-book's 'spicy breezes'
blowing soft over Ceylon. But
whereas, in that island, 'every
prospect pleases and only man is vile,'
here he is merely absent.

Jerez de los Caballeros Not to be
confused with the sherry capital in
Andalucía, this little Extremadurian
town owes its name to the Knights
Templars, the *caballeros* who wrested
it from the Moors in 1230, and its
renown to the great conquistador
Nuñez de Balboa who was born here.
To whom it owes its Baroque belfries
is unknown, and the anonymity only
adds to the mystery of their profusion
and exuberance.

Rioja Even the best Spanish wines are not in the same league as the *grands crus* of Bordeaux, but in terms of value for money they are beyond compare. (Alas, it is hard to avoid this sort of salesman's talk when discussing them.) What else can account for the popularity of, say, Rioja, which in recent years has become as much of a household word as claret? A vineyard in harvest-time is a joy, no matter where, and in Spain where more primitive conditions prevail – transport is still by cart as well as by truck – bucolic gaiety and rustic mirth are second nature.

Eastern Spain

he former principality of Catalonia, arguably the most 'foreign' of all the Spains, perhaps ought to have a section to itself. Here it is tucked into the eastern region together with the kingdoms of Valencia and Murcia. They are not such bad bedfellows, after all.

When Franco's Moorish troops stormed into Barcelona at the end of the Civil War, they ordered the inhabitants to 'speak Christian now' instead of their native tongue. This was tantamount to blasphemy; to the Catalans their language was sacred, and its reinstatement immediately after the Caudillo's death was akin to a religious revival. Even today it is something more to them than a means of communication; it is a symbol of their independence from Madrid; it reinforces their sense of belonging to the Mediterranean more than to the Peninsula; it contributes to their feeling of kinship with the Midi of France rather than with other parts of Spain. Commerce with the East enriched med-ieval Barcelona and did something for the character of her citizens. In contrast to the hidalgos *of Castile, whose code demanded contempt for money in general and the earning of it in particular, Catalan merchants were not above making fortunes and preferred a respected trade-mark to a coat of arms. There was an element in their nature which they called* seny *– untranslatable but meaning something like commonsense, gumption or judgement, the quality of having one's head screwed on the right way – and this they have handed down to their descendants.*

Catalan is spoken in Valencia, too, though the locals prefer to call it Valencian. But there the resemblance to Catalonia ends. If the latter conjures up factories and dark satanic mills (which in reality are confined to the outskirts of Barcelona) the former evokes a limitless expanse of orange groves, a veritable Garden of the Hesperides. In Murcia you are back among Castilian-speakers, though from the looks of it you would expect to hear Arabic. The countryside, apart from the cultivated vegas, *is African. So, too, beneath a Baroque façade, is the provincial capital itself. And where else would you come across without surprise the biggest forest of date-palms in Europe?*

Aigües Tortes The name, 'Winding Waters', denotes the nature of the landscape. This national park on the border between Catalonia and Aragón is a labyrinth of streams and lakes hemmed in by wooded slopes and rocky crags. It is no place for a genuine mountaineer but is perfect for a mountain walker, being wild enough in appearance to give him a sense of pioneering but in reality so tame, thanks to a network of paths and tracks, that he can crisscross the area effortlessly in every direction.

Barcelona By the middle of the last century Barcelona had become Spain's gateway to the Mediterranean, and the consequent population explosion led to a building boom. The moat was filled in to make room for a ring of broad boulevards, and handsome new avenues radiated into the countryside. The medieval houses in the centre were also pulled down, but only to be replaced by tenements which, soaring from the existing foundations, transformed the narrow lanes into urban chasms. People from all over Spain have crowded into this district, so it is no surprise to come across an Andalucían café decorated with flamenco posters and frequented by clients wearing the regional *sombrero ancho*.

The Ramblas The wide open spaces of Barcelona's squares and boulevards are a boon to the pavement artist. But it's the Ramblas, the famous avenue lined with booths selling flowers and exotic birds, that attracts the tourist; while the latter, conspicuous in dress and in behaviour, attracts the attention of the native.

Barcelona Cathedral By all means admire the handsome façade in full sunlight, but do not then step inside straight away. Barcelona is even darker than most Spanish cathedrals, so allow your eyes a minute or two to accustom themselves to the gloom; or else postpone your visit till the evening and benefit from electric light. The cloister is worth more than a glance at any time of the day. It is an oasis of greenery and sparkling waters in a desert of carved stone. Don't forget to toss a ritualistic crust to the geese floating on the pond. They are grossly overfed but not likely to be turned into *foie gras*, being as sacred as their forebears on the Roman Capitol.

Barcelona: The Sagrada Familia

The Church of the Holy Family is a vision in more senses than one – something in the nature of a revelation, the product of a highly developed imagination, and something of such unusual appearance as to make the beholder unable to believe his eyes. The most ambitious brain-child of the modernist architect Antoni Gaudí, it also stands as a symbol of Catalan nationalism. Work on it was suspended during the Franco régime, when the Catalan language was likewise banned; and it remains unfinished to this day, a gantry crane still brooding over the fretted towers. These have been likened to giant pretzel sticks studded with salt crystals and the rest of the structure invites equally unflattering comparisons. But, whether an aberration or a work of genius, it cannot be regarded with indifference.

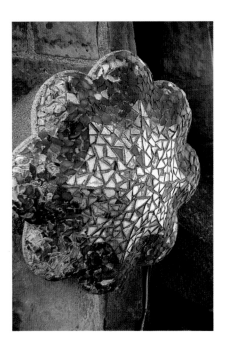

The Casa Batlló Besides the Sagrada Familia, many other Barcelona buildings and even the pavements (*below*) bear the unmistakable Gaudí stamp. The Parque Güell is a pre-Raphaelite Disneyland where you half expect to see the Seven Dwarfs pop up and perform a Morris dance. The Milá apartment house is a miniature Montserrat, with undulating balconies to suggest the mountain's contours. The nearby Casa Batlló (*right*) seems to have been inspired by Hokusai's woodcut of the Great Wave. The walls surge wildly upwards like a Pacific breaker, its foam and spray represented by the cresting of green tiles on the roof. What the chimney-pot symbolizes is anyone's guess.

Montserrat (*following pages*) The 'sawtooth mountain' has attracted pilgrims for centuries. Some come to worship at the shrine of *La Moreneta*, the Catalan counterpart of Our Lady of Guadalupe. Others identify it as the legendary Monsalvat, depicted in Wagner's *Parsifal* as the hiding place of the Holy Grail. There are others still who simply come for the sake of the landscape, which is 'horrid' in every sense. The peaks resemble a giant's mandible, the teeth so carious that if a dentist were to find their like in a human mouth he would advise having the whole lot out at once.

The Eastern Shore Mass tourism has been a mixed blessing to Spain, filling her coffers but ruining much of her coastline. Fishing villages have been degraded into jerry-built Manhattans, virgin beaches raped by developers with an eye for the fast buck. Luckily there are exceptions and, as long as places like Calella de Palafrugell (*inset*) are spared the worst outrages, the Costa Brava, or 'Wild Coast,' will not entirely belie its name. Compare it to Benidorm, further south on the Costa Blanca, where the Statue of Liberty would not look out of place amongst the skyscrapers.

Gastronomy Despite competition from supermarkets that have lately sprung up all over the country, the classical Spanish market-places still hold their own. The best are the old-fashioned ones, lofty edifices of glass and metal built about the same date as London's Crystal Palace, which they often resemble in dimension and design. Stall upon stall of colourful fecundity give promise of culinary delights peculiar to every region. Spain's reputation for poor food is undeserved. Avoid the 'international cuisine' intended for the tourist. Stick to the local dishes. You'll be pleasantly surprised.

The Fallas of Valencia (*preceding pages*) If you find yourself in Valencia on 19 March, be forewarned. It is the feast of St Joseph and, as you know, St Joseph was a carpenter. What you may not know is that on that day, in the Middle Ages, Valencian carpenters made bonfires of their sweepings and shavings. As time went by they took to manufacturing what they planned to burn, and the tradition continues. Grotesque pasteboard effigies are now destined for the flames; after a while you get used to them being perambulated up and down the streets. What comes as a surprise is the fireworks display, as loud and prolonged as an artillery barrage, which heralds their midnight combustion.

Dry-goods The commercial synonym for drapery and the like could be more appropriately applied to the wide range of dehydrated foodstuffs available in Spain. Here are two samples. Carpets of pimientos are spread out to dry, forming *sang-de-boeuf* patches in the landscape, and octopuses hang on a laundry line like the 'smalls' of a Charles Addams family.

Fans They once formed an integral part of an elegant woman's wardrobe, complementing the *mantilla* and *peineta* (comb). In skilful hands they could serve several purposes: a flirtatious young lady might handle one as an instrument of coquetry, and her *dueña* might call her to order by rapping her over the knuckles with another. They could also, of course, be used in the manner for which they were intended – to stir the air and produce a breeze – and they still can be. But, amongst the young at any rate, they are no longer fashionable: blue jeans and unisex sartorial gimmicks are putting paid to them.

Southern Spain

The last four kingdoms of Spain – Seville, Córdoba, Jaén and Granada – were not Spanish at all; they were the Moorish divisions of the southernmost part of the country to which the Vandals lent their name. What is now known as Andalucía corresponds closely to the popular image of Spain: the operatic Spain of Verdi and Bizet, the romantic Spain of Mérimée and Washington Irving, the jet-set Spain of the international gossip-columnist, the 'sea and sand and sunshine' Spain of the tour operator and travel agent.

To the Moors this territory was Lotus-land and during their occupation, while the rest of Europe wallowed in superstition and barbarism, Andalucía took the lead in every branch of intellectual and artistic pursuit. Yet one after another the kingdoms fell to reconquering Spanish armies.

Granada was the last to go, and the defeated King Boabdil wept as he looked back for the last time at his beloved Alhambra. His mother's reproach has gone down in history. 'you may well weep like a woman,' she said, 'for what you did not defend like a man.' Charles V's comment is less well known but no less apt. 'She was right,' he said, 'for a tomb in the Alhambra is better than a palace in the Alpujarras' (where the Catholic Monarchs decreed Boabdil was to live in exile). No sooner was the Christian banner floating over the Muslim towers than the rot set in. What were once Elysian fields flowing with oil and wine, relapsed into depopulated wastes, and by the end of the eighteenth century Andalucía had become the poorest and most backward region in Spain (and for that reason perhaps the most picturesque). The tourist industry has since improved the standard of living, but not necessarily the quality of life.

Bullfighting Many may call this a cruel sport, but as any Spaniard will tell you, it is not a sport at all. It is an art, a national institution, a spectacle of such dramatic intensity that the cruelty involved is irrelevant. The bullfight is as formal as Greek tragedy, and governed by rules as rigid as those of the classical theatre. There is no departure from tradition; and just as the climax of the play is predetermined, so the outcome of the *corrida* is a foregone conclusion. But

the ritual continues to evolve: a glance at a Goya print will show how it has developed since his day. New passes have been invented, new techniques introduced: for instance when sighting for the *verónica,* which used to be made from the frontal postition, the matador nowadays stands sideways to the bull. Though wishful thinkers have long been predicting its imminent end, the *arte del toreo* is alive and flourishing.

Seville: The Plaza de España
(*preceding pages*) Seville's Golden
Age began with Christopher
Columbus' discovery of the New World
and rose to its height in the sixteenth
century. A river of gold flowed
upstream into the city in which the
Catholic Monarchs held court. In the
market-place outside the cathedral,
emeralds and other precious stones
were bought and sold like beans, by
the sackful. But two centuries of
prodigal spending reduced the

seemingly inexhaustible flood of
treasure to a trickle, the Guadalquivir
silted up, and the reduced river port
took second place to the deep-water
harbour of Cadiz. The Great
Exhibition of 1929, however, put
Seville back on the map. The city
fathers built a monumental square in
which to house the exhibits, dredged
the river, and reopened the docks to
shipping. The Plaza de España is a
durable symbol of Seville's continuing
prosperity.

Seville Cathedral It is only right and
proper that Columbus, who was
responsible for Seville's affluence,
should be laid to rest in Seville
cathedral. His tomb, representing an
immense coffin inscribed with his
name and carried by four more-than-
lifesize regal figures symbolising the
kingdoms of León, Castilla, Navarra
and Aragón, is as massive as can be;
yet the immensity of the surroundings
reduces it almost to insignificance.
This cathedral, built on the site of a
former mosque, is the largest in
Spain, and one of the most grandiose
and solemn.

Seville: The Giralda Cathedral bells now toll where once the *muezzin* called to prayer. The former minaret, built at the same time and on the same scale as the Hassan tower at Rabat and the Koutoubia of Marrakesh, eventually outgrew them both. Victorious Christians added to the twelfth-century Moorish structure, first of all by piling on a belfry, then on top of this a lantern, and finally a thirteen-foot-tall bronze statue of Faith holding a banner which catches the wind and acts as a weather vane, sending the statue spinning – whence its name, Giralda (from the Spanish *girar* – to spin), which later came to be applied to the tower itself, Seville's best known and most easily discernible landmark.

Seville: The Alcazar The fortified palace known as the Alcazar (*left*), though Moorish in name and unmistakably Moorish in design, was in fact built by a Spanish king in the mid fourteenth century, a hundred years after the Reconquest. Pedro de Castilla was on the best of terms with the Moorish kings still ruling in Granada, and the recently completed Alhambra inspired him to construct something similar in Seville. The result is this outstanding example of Mudéjar architecture, that essentially Iberian blend of Christian and Islamic styles. The same delightful fusion of European and Arab traditions is apparent in the palace of the dukes of Medinaceli (*right*) commonly called the Casa de Pilatos, 'Pilate's House' because it is popularly believed to copy many of the features of the Biblical Pilate's house in Jerusalem. No words can do justice to this jewel of a dwelling. It defies description.

Holy Week Only a bigoted atheist
could take exception to Holy Week in
Seville or Granada, which nowadays
owes as much to tradition as to
religious belief. Not every cowled and
hooded figure is a heartfelt penitent,
but at least he is properly dressed for
the occasion. The effigies of the Virgin
that are carried shoulder-high
through the streets are obviously not
flesh and blood, but, as custom
demands, they are treated as though
they were. Men blow kisses at them
and shower them with compliments;
women let fly with a *saeta*, an
impromptu 'arrow of song', as their
favourite is trundled past. Is this
mariolatry, the idolatrous worship of
Our Lady? Certainly, and where's the
harm in that?

The Feria The *feria* that succeeds Holy Week in Seville is not so much a fair as a three-day festival in which the whole population takes part. There is something in it for everyone: singing and dancing, feasting and drinking, fireworks and bullfights. What makes it unique is the endless equestrian parade, a perfect opportunity for exhibitionism. The cavaliers display their horsemanship, their steeds are put through their paces, but it's the girls who steal the show – girls riding pillion, perched precariously with an arm round their partner's waist or holding on to the horse's tail, wearing flounced skirts as full as crinolines, and looking even lovelier than they actually are.

The Sierra Nevada No wonder the Moors felt at home within sight of the Sierra Nevada; it must have reminded them of their snow-capped Atlas. They took advantage of this perpetual source of fertilizing water to turn the *vega* of Granada into a semi-tropical paradise. Motor roads and ski resorts have robbed the range of its mystery, but its beauty remains unchanged and unchangeable.

Granada For most people Granada is a mere antechamber to the Alhambra, a place you have to go through to reach the Holy of Holies on top of one of the town's three hills. But Granada also has something to say for itself, and so do the other two hills. On the Sacromonte you can pay through the nose for a flamenco song-and-dance routine performed *chez l'habitant* by a cave-dwelling gypsy. On the Albaicín you are back to the Muslim world, in a maze of little lanes lined with *carmen* after *carmen* (the name, peculiar to Granada, for the sort of Moorish villa that inspired Manuel de Falla's delicate orchestral suite *Noches en los jardines de España*) and Granada itself is not only the burial place of the Catholic Monarchs; it was also the home-town of poet and playwright Federico García Lorca.

The Alhambra (*preceding pages*)
This must be one of the most
spectacular views in the world: the red
walls and towers of the Alhambra
covering the hills above the deep
gorge of the Darro, with the Sierra
Nevada in the background.

The Alhambra The wonder of this
Moorish palace is that anything so
flimsy could have lasted so long.
Constructed in the fourteenth century,
it was not built for posterity. Where
you would expect stone, you find
brick; what looks like marble turns
out to be stucco; much of the
construction is of lathe and plaster.
Architecture here takes second place
to decoration. But what decoration!
Cellular stalactites hang from the
ceilings like wasps' nests, and
geometrical designs and ornamental
inscriptions invade every wall, in such
profusion and of such intricacy that
they seem to be less the work of man
than a masterpiece produced by
artistic insects. By comparison the
Dionysian head, part of a sixteenth-
century fountain close to one of the
main gates, is only too solid and too
human.

The Generalife Water, water
everywhere, enough to slake the thirst
of ten thousand Ancient Mariners all
at once. Water in cascades and in
canals, in fountains and in rills.
Water exploding like a firework
display from avenues of brass nozzles,
or mysteriously gurgling in the depths
of artificial grottoes. Nowhere else in
Spain has the element been more
effectively used than in the gardens of
the Generalife, the summer palace of
the Moors which adjoins the
Alhambra.

The Great Mosque of Córdoba.
The most picturesque approach to the ancient *Mezquita-Catedral* is across the Roman Bridge over the Guadalquivir. The forecourt, planted with orange trees, is disappointing – unless you are here in orange-blossom time. Then the scent you are still inhaling as you enter the building will contribute to the illusion of being wafted on a perfumed cloud into an enchanted forest. In reality the trees are elegant columns of marble and granite, jasper and onyx, some topped with Roman and Byzantine capitals, others with capitals salvaged from the Visigothic church that stood on the site before the present edifice rose under the enlightened rule of the caliphs. Another church – a whole cathedral in fact – was inserted into the precinct in the reign of Charles V. But such is the scale of the great mosque, so captivating each individual feature, that you may not even notice the ugly Christian blot on the serene Islamic landscape.

Ronda (*preceding pages*) These
houses clustering like martins' nests
along the edge of the cliff have a
bird's eye view of eagles soaring far
below.

Ronda Once a fashionable hill
station, the Simla or Ootacamund of
Andalucía, Ronda now depends for its
clientèle on package tours from
abroad and day excursions from the
coast. Perched on the edge of a steep
escarpment and on both sides of a
dramatic gorge, it also balances on a
watershed between two worlds. The
half-envied, half-despised Sodoms
and Gomorrahs of the Costa del Sol
are tantalisingly close; but closer still
is the familiar Shangri-La of the
sierras and *pueblos*. May there never
be any doubt as to which of these
worlds will eventually prevail.

Ronda's Bullring As befits 'the cradle of the modern bullfight,' – it was here that Pedro Romero, born in 1698, invented the red cloth *muleta* – Ronda's *plaza de toros* is unique. It was not designed as a bullring at all, but as a riding-school for the nobility. This accounts for the size of the circular sanded area, one of the largest in the country, and the relatively small seating capacity. It also accounts for the beauty of the architecture and for a certain aura of rusticity. If many arenas in Spain can be equated with cathedrals, then Ronda's is a rural parish church. Rustic elegance is not limited to the bullring. It is evident in architectural features all over Ronda, especially in the old part known as *la ciudad*.

Tabernas Parts of Spain look almost too cinematic to be true. Inland from Almería, between Benahadux and Tabernas, you might fancy yourself in the Wild West of the early movie-makers. Just off the main road there is even a typical one-horse town, complete with saloon and sheriff's office. A mirage? No, but something only a little less unsubstantial – a film set. If you think you have seen it before, you probably have. It must have starred in every spaghetti western to have been produced in Europe during the last twenty years.

The White Pueblos These villages act as punctuation marks in the dense paragraphs of the Andalucían *sierras*. The landscape would be illegible without them. In short, they make sense. They are also individually beautiful, and beautifully individualistic. To the foreign eye there may be little to choose between them, but each is as conscious of its own superiority as any Highland clan. The loyalty they engender in their inhabitants is akin to patriotism of the fiercest kind; for a man's *pueblo* is not only his home but also his homeland.

The Southern Shore Like most of
Spain's Mediterranean littoral, the
Costa del Sol has suffered irreparable
damage from developers' short-
sightedness and speculators' greed.
But take heart: the Atlantic shore,
west of Tarifa, remains more or less
unscathed. Colder ocean waters and
stronger winds deter the crowds;
foreign visitors do not yet outnumber
the local inhabitants; the wind-
surfers, drawn here by the ideal
conditions, impinge not at all but
provide flashes of colour as timely
and appropriate as the burgees and
pennants of a Dufy seascape.

The Coto de Doñana This area of marshland and sand dunes at the mouth of the Guadalquivir is one of the largest and richest wildlife reserves in Europe. For centuries it has been a refuge for deer and foxes, lynxes and wildboar, and even wild camels, to name but a few of the animals to be found there. As for the birds, their species are legion. Now all these creatures are at risk. Plans to turn the Coto into a tourist resort were fortunately shelved, but not before a settlement was built for 150,000 holiday-makers. Concrete towers have risen not far from where flamingoes nest, and sewage spills into the sea. The full effect of this vandalism remains to be felt.

Jerez or Sherry Like champagne, the wine is synonymous with its birthplace. *Albariza*, the best sherry soil, sometimes looks like molten gold, sometimes like clay. In winter it acts as a sponge, soaking up every drop of moisture. In summer it goes rock-hard on the surface, sealed by the furnace of the sun. But down below, at root level, the vines imbibe from their subterranean reservoirs, enabling the fresh green leaves and plump jade grapes to flourish in the incandescent atmosphere above. The result of this magical process is, as it should be, unique.

Island Spain

fter citing so many former kingdoms within the Peninsula, I am tempted to mention the Balearics as an example of one off shore. But I must resist. The islands were never a kingdom on their own; they only formed part of the one that James I of Aragón created by amalgamating them with his French possessions after driving the Moors out of Majorca.

The archipelago's landscape, architecture and climate could not be more varied. Georges Sand and Frédéric Chopin, who spent the winter of 1838 in Majorca, did nothing but complain of the weather and the discomfort of their quarters in the deconsecrated charterhouse of Valldemosa. They might have fared better had they rented one of the many Italianate mansions in Palma, or moved to another island altogether. In Minorca they would have found houses with sash-windows and rocking-chairs – legacies of the eighteenth-century British occupation – but the winds that ravage these low-lying shores would have given cause for further complaint. Ibiza's sugar-cube villages might have reminded them of the Cyclades, but not appealed to them for any other reason. As a last resort they might have gone native in Formentera, but found no adequate dwelling on this mere spit of sand or even enough room for the piano.

I wonder what they would have made of the Canaries. When the Spaniards landed here in the fifteenth century they found a native population still living in the Stone Age. Finding also spring-time weather all year round, they joined the ancients in lauding these 'Islands of the Blest.' Was this archipelago off the coast of Africa perhaps a remnant of the drowned continent, Atlantis? Lanzarote's lunar landscape, Tenerife's volcanic cone, and the world's largest crater on La Palma certainly suggest some giant cataclysm. For me this unsolved mystery, this slightly sinister element, enhances the Canaries' allure.

Ibiza Housing developments and tourist resorts are spreading like psoriasis over the Balearics. Concrete pustules already disfigure the coastline and threaten to infect the interior. The smaller islands are of course at greater risk. So far the disease has spared Ibiza's distinctive architecture, a blend of archaic and oriental. The whitewashed churches would not look out of place in the Aegean; the village lanes are as labyrinthine as a Moroccan *medina*. The only visible concessions to modernity in the old houses are water-pipes and electric cables attached to the outside walls with blithe indifference to rectilinearity.

Ibiza The hinterland remains relatively unspoilt. In some parts the original *norias* introduced by the Moors are still used for irrigation, and manual labourers work the fields where tractors fear to tread. There are peasants still, but only just. The older women dress, according to tradition, in long pleated skirt and dark shawl and kerchief, with one plait of hair hanging down behind. They may well be the last generation to do so.

Palma (*preceding pages*) Majorca will never be entirely spoilt while the centre of the capital remains as it is. The old town of Palma is an oasis of dignity and refinement in a desert of commercialism and vulgarisation. Mansion after well-preserved mansion testify to the island's opulence from the beginning of the fifteenth to the end of the sixteenth century, when the cathedral, started three hundred years before, was finally completed. This superb Gothic edifice was, and still is, visible for miles out at sea, rising from the waves like some Mediterranean Chartres from a miraculously liquified Plaine de la Beauce.

Lanzarote The only way to grow anything in Lanzarote is to scoop out the all-enveloping lava, fill the dip with *picón*, or volcanic dust, and sow it or plant it as though it was soil. In the absence of permanent springs and constant rain, the *picón* absorbs whatever moisture is available. Only the salt-pans provide relief from the universal blackness of the landscape.

Lanzarote The most easterly of the Canaries has been visibly in mourning since the early eighteenth century, when a six-year-long series of volcanic eruptions turned its fertile fields into a sea of lava and shrouded them in widow's weeds of ash. The island now bristles with volcanic cones; and formations of petrified lava, blood-red and sulphurous, attitudinise against the carbonised background. Appropriately, dromedaries as well as jeeps are used to transport visitors across this scorched terrain. Certain spots are so hot that steak or sucking-pig can be barbecued simply by being laid on the ground. In Lanzarote even the beaches are black, and along the coast there are lagoons even denser and more saline than the Dead Sea.

Tenerife Tucked away in the western half of the archipelago, Tenerife is the loveliest of the Canaries, with the greatest variety of scenery. There is one spot on the north coast that is said to have brought the German naturalist Baron von Humboldt to his knees in admiration. This part of the island is indeed the most fertile, with orange groves and banana plantations carpeting the slopes almost to sea level. In the south, African winds have created a miniature Sahara. The central plateau is something else again: a landscape half Alpine, half volcanic. Mists often hover over the ancient crater of Las Cañadas, a wilderness of black and red lava tufted with giant broom (and seen *right* dusted with winter snow), from the midst of which soars, phoenix-like, the great cone of the Pico del Teide.

Canary Island Beaches

Fuerteventura, the second largest of
the Canaries and the nearest to Africa,
was once a scrubby wilderness fit only
for goats and for those 'fiancés of
death', the Foreign Legion. But now
the legionaries have gone and shock-
troops of developers have taken the
island by storm in advance of the
plodding package-tour battalions.
Vast stretches of golden sand are not
enough for them; they have to have
concrete-lined swimming-pools as
well. How long will it be, I wonder,
before the dunes of Maspalomas in
neighbouring Gran Canaria are
likewise tamed into submission.

Index

Figures in *italics* refer to captions

Aigües Tortes (national park), *61*
Ainsa, *22*
Albaicín, *102*
Albariza, *127*
Alcazar Palace, (Seville), *94*
Alhambra, 85, *94, 102, 106, 109*
Alloza, *24*
Almería, *119*
Alpujarras, 85
Andalucía, 9-10, *54,* 85, *115, 120*
Asturias, 13, *18*

Balboa, Nuñez de, *54*
Balearic Islands, 13, 129, *130*
Barcelona, 7, 8, 11, 59, *63-9, 70*
Barcelona Cathedral, *66*
Basque Region, 9, 13
Bay of Biscay, *20*
Benahadux, *119*
Benidorm, *70*
Bilbao, *20*
Boabdil, King, 85
bullfighting, *87, 117*
bullrunning, *28*

Cadiz, *90*
Calella de Palafrugell, *75*
Cañadas, Las, *140*
Canary Islands, 13, 124, *138, 140,
143*
Cantabrian mountains, 13, *18*
Casa Batlló, (Barcelona), *70*
Casa de Pilatos (Pilate's House), *94*
Castile, 33, *39,* 59
Castilla-la Mancha, 33
Castilla-León, 33

Castro Urdiales, *20*
Catalonia, 8, 59, *61*
Cazorla, 10
Cervantes Saavedra, Miguel de, *47*
Charles V, King, 85, *111*
Córdoba, 85, *111*
Costa Blanca, *75*
Costa Brava, *75*
Costa del Sol, *115, 123*
Coto de Doñana, (national park)
124
cuidad, la, 117

Darro, *106*
dry-goods, *81*

east coast, *75*
Ebro Valley, *4, 24*
Escorial, the, *41*
Estanque, 39
Extremadura, 33, *47, 54*

Fallas of Valencia, *81*
fans, *82*
Feast of St. Joseph, *81*
Feria de San Fermín, *28*
Feria of Seville, *99*
food, *77, 81*
Formentera, 129
Franco, General, 6, 10, 11, 59, *69*
Fuerteventura, *143*

Galicia, 9, 13
gastronomy, *77*
Gaudí, Antoni, *69, 70*
Generalife, the, *93*
Gran Canaria, *143*

Granada, 85, 94, *97, 100, 102*
Great Central Plain, *47*
Great Mosque of Córdoba, *111*
Guadalquivir River, *90, 111, 124*
Guadalupe, *50*
Guadiana, 33

Holy Week, *97*

Ibiza, 129, *130, 133*

Jaén, 85
James I of Aragon, King, 129
Jerez, *127*

La Mancha, 9, *47*
La Moreneta (Guadalupe), *70*
Lanzarote, 129, *136, 138*
León, 9
Lorca, Federico García, *102*

Madrid, 129, *136*
Majorca, 34, *36,* 59
Maria Christina, Queen, *29*
Maspalomas, 143
Mezquita-Catedral, (Córdoba), *111*
Milá house, *70*
Minorca, 129
Murcia, 59

Navarra, 13
norias, 133

Palma, Majorca, *136*
Pamplona, *28*
Parque Güell, (Barcelona), *70*
Pedro de Castilla, King, *94*
Philip II, King, *94*
Pico del Teide, *140*

Picos de Europa, *18*
Pilate's House, (Seville), *94*
Plaza de España, (Seville), *90*
Pyrenees, 13, *27*

Ramblas, the, (Barcelona), *64*
Retiro, the, (Madrid), *39*
Rioja, la, *4, 56*
Romero, Pedro, *117*
Roncesvalles, 13
Ronda, *115, 117*

Sacromonte, *102*
Sagrada Familia (Barcelona), *69*
San Sebastián, *29*
San Vicente, *4*
Santander, *20*
Santiago de Compostela, 13, *14, 17*
Segovia, *42*
Seville, 11, 85, *90-5, 97*
Seville Cathedral, *90, 93, 99*
sherry, *127*
Sierra Nevada, *100, 106*

Tabernas, *119*
Tarifa, *123*
Tenerife, 129, *140*
Toledo, *51*

Valencia, 9, 59, *81*
Valldemosa, 129

Way of St. James, the, 13, 14
White Pueblos, *120*

Acknowledgements

The Publishers would like to thank the following organisations and individuals for their kind permission to reproduce the photographs in this book:

A.G.E. 20, 21, 24, 25, 30-31, 48-49, 58, 62, 67, 70 top, 71, 74, 76, 76-77, 77 right, 104-105, 138-139. **Ardea London Ltd.** Bob Gibbons 26; / F Gohier 27; / A Lindau 125. **Cephas Picture Library** / Mick Rock 56, 56-57, 126-127. **Jonathan Chester / Extreme Images** 32, 50, 66, 64, 65, 70 bottom, 72-73, 78 top, 78 bottom, 79, 83, 89 inset, 90, 91, 92, 93, 95, 102, 103, 106 top, 107, 108, 109, 116, 117, 123. **Robert Harding Picture Library** 82, 130-131, 134-135; / R Francis 81. **Hutchison Library** 140; / J Downman 1; / P Goycolea 16. **Landscape Only** 4-5, 50-51; / T Chadget 118 right; / G Kiernan 38-39. **Magnum Photos Ltd.** / B Barbey 14, 17; /I Berry 63; / S Franklin 6; / H Gruyaert 29, 52-53, 54-55;/ Ernst Haas front endpaper, 10-11 / F Scianna 98, 99; / D Stock 142. **Robert O'Dea** 84, 106 bottom. **Pictures Colour Library** 34-35, 141. **Rex Features Ltd.** 39; / Beirne 28; / NJP Jorgensen 36; / Sipa Press 15. **Spectrum** 12, 22, 22-23, 40-41, 41, 44-45, 46, 47, 69 top right, 69 bottom, 74-75, 86 left, 86 right, 87 right, 94, 97, 100-101, 101 bottom, 110, 111 left, 111 right, 112-113, 114, 115, 119 right, 120-121, 122, 124, 130, 132, 136, 136-137; / J Aston 120; / D Ball 68; / M Dubin 18, 19; / Dallas & John Heaton 88-89; / C Hewitt 60-61; / J Kugler 42, 42-43. **Zefa** 8-9, back endpaper, 96, 128, 143; / K Benser 80; / Braennhage 37.